Baráye

آری عليا وَ میلی

Árie, Alíá & Mílly

May you always find
comfort & solace in the Divine.

"Meditation is the key for
opening the doors of mysteries."

'Abdú'l-Bahá

Dear Reader,

To assist you in deciphering the alphabet we have
included the short vowels in the text to help sound out new words.
You will find our Alphabet letter guide &
Pronunciation guide at the back of the book
which may assist you in decoding difficult and unfamiliar words.

Out of respect for the Sacred origins of the
Persian & Arabic Prayers compiled in this publication,
a transliteration has not been provided.
You can find all prayers here https://www.bahai.org/library/

Download our Digital Poster
Bahá'í Persian Alphabet guide printable for quick reference:
Go to this link and use free code.

CODE: BAHAIPRAYER

If you have ideas, suggestions or feedback to facilitate learning or
to make Persian more accessible for the Iranian diaspora, I would love to hear from you:
englisifarsi@gmail.com

Be umídi dídár,
Moná مُنا

Contents

English & Persian [Fársí]

He is God! O God, my God!	Page 5
O my Lord! O my Lord! I am a child…	Page 6
O Thou peerless Lord! Let this suckling babe…	Page 7
O Lord! I am a child: enable me to grow…	Page 8
O Thou kind Lord! These lovely children…	Page 9
O Lord! Make this youth radiant…	Page 10
He is God! O Lord! How shall we thank Thee?	Page 11

English & Arabic [A'rabí]

O Lord! Thou are the Remover of every anguish	Page 14
Is there any Remover of difficulties…	Page 15

Alphabet Guides

Pronunciation Guide	Page 16
Persian Alphabet	Page 17
Persian Alphabet Letter Guide	Page 18 & 19

Persian
Fársí
فارسی

He is God!

O God, my God! Bestow upon me a pure heart, like unto a pearl.

'Abdu'l-Bahá

هوَاللّه

پَروَردِگارا،

قَلبِ صافی چون دُرّ عطا فَرما.

ع ع

O my Lord! O my Lord! I am a child of tender years. Nourish me from the breast of Thy mercy, train me in the bosom of Thy love, educate me in the school of Thy guidance and develop me under the shadow of Thy bounty. Deliver me from darkness, make me a brilliant light; free me from unhappiness, make me a flower of the rose garden; suffer me to become a servant of Thy threshold, and confer upon me the disposition and nature of the righteous; make me a cause of bounty to the human world, and crown my head with the diadem of eternal life. Verily, Thou art the Powerful, the Mighty, the Seer, the Hearer.

'Abdu'l-Bahá

هوَاَّلله

رَبّی ، رَبّی، کودَکَم خُردسال از پِستانِ عِنایَت شیر ده وَ دَر آغوشِ مُحَبَّتَت پَروَرِش بَخش وَ دَر دَبِستانِ هِدایَت تَعلیم فَرما وَ دَر ظِلّ عِنایَتَت تَربیَت کُن. از تاریکی بِرَهان، شَمعِ روشَن کُن. از پَژمُردگی نِجات ده گُل گُلشَن فَرما. بَندۀ آستان کُن وَ خُلق وَ خوی راستان بَخش. مُوهِبَتِ عالَمِ اِنسانی کُن وَ تاجی از حَیاتِ اَبَدیّه بَر سَر نِه. تویی مُقتَدِر وَ تَوانا وَ تویی شِنَوَنده وَ بینا.

ع ع

O Thou peerless Lord! Let this sucking babe be nursed from the breast of Thy loving-kindness, guard it within the cradle of Thy safety and protection and grant that it be reared in the arms of Thy tender affection.

'Abdu'l-Bahá

هوالله

ای خُداوندِ بی مانَند، این طِفلِ شیرخوار را اَز پِستانِ عنایَت شیر دِه وَ دَر مَهدِ صون وَ حِمایَت مَحفوظ وَ مَصون دار وَ دَر آغوشِ اَلطاف پَروَرِش دِه.

ع ع

O Lord! I am a child; enable me to grow beneath the shadow of Thy loving-kindness. I am a tender plant; cause me to be nurtured through the outpourings of the clouds of Thy bounty. I am a sapling of the garden of love; make me into a fruitful tree.
Thou are the Might and the Powerful, and Thou are the All-Loving, the All-knowing, the All-Seeing.

'Abdu'l-Bahá

هوالله

خُدایا طِفلَم دَر ظِلِّ عِنایَتَت پَرْوَرِش دِه. نَهالِ تازه ام بِرَشحاتِ سَحابِ عِنایَت پَرْوَرِش فَرما. گیاهِ حَدیقهٔ مُحَبَّتم دِرَختِ بارْوَر کُن. توئی مُقتَدِر وَ تَوانا وَ توئی مِهرَبان وَ دانا وَ بینا.

ع ع

O Thou kind Lord! These lovely children are the handiwork of the fingers of Thy might and the wonderous signs of Thy greatness. O God! Protect these children, graciously assist them to be educated and enable them to render service to the world of humanity. O God! These children are pearls, cause them to be nurtured within the shell of Thy loving-kindness.
Thou art the Bountiful, the All-Loving.

'Abdu'l-Bahá

هوَاللّه

ای خُداوَندِ مِهرَبان این أطفالِ نازَنین صُنعِ دَستِ قُدرَتِ تواند وَ آیاتِ عَظِمَتِ تو خُدایا این کودَکان را مَحفوظ بدار.

مُوَیَّد بَر تعَلیم کُن وَ مُوَفَّق بخدمَتِ عالَمِ اِنسانی فَرما.

خُدایا این اَطفال دُردانِه اند دَر آغوشِ صَدَفِ عِنایَت پَرورِش دِه توئی بَخشَندِه وَ مِهرَبان.

ع ع

O Lord! Make this youth radiant, and confer Thy bounty upon this poor creature. Bestow upon him knowledge, grant him added strength at the break of every morn and guard him within the shelter of Thy protection so that he may be freed from error, may devote himself to the service of Thy Cause, may guide the wayward, lead the hapless, free the captives and awaken the heedless, that all may be blessed with Thy remembrance and praise. Thou art the Mighty and the Powerful.

'Abdu'l-Bahá

هوَاللّه

ای پَروَردِگار این نوجَوان را نورانی کُن وَ این بینَوا را نَوایی بَخش وَ آگاهی عَطا فَرما وَ دَر هَر صُبحگاهی مَدَدِ جَدیدی بَخش. تا دَر پَناهِ تو از هَر گُناهی مَحفوظ وَ مَصون مانَد وَ بخِدمَتِ اَمرَت پَردازَد. گُمراهان را هِدایَت فَرمایَد وَ بیچارِگان را دِلالَت کُنَد. اَسیران را آزاد نَمایَد وَ غافِلان را بیدار کُنَد وَ بِیاد وَ ذِکرَت دَمساز شَوَند. تویی مُقتَدِر وَ تَوانا

ع ع

He is God! O Lord! How shall we thank Thee? Thy bounties are limitless, and our gratitude but limited. How can the limited render thanks to the limitless? Incapable are we of offering thanks for Thy mercies. Utterly powerless, we turn unto Thy Kingdom, and beg Thee to increase Thy bestowal and bounty. Thou art the Giver, Thou are the Bestower, Thou art the Powerful.

'Abdu'l-Bahá

هوالله

خُداوَندا چِگونِه تو را شُکر نَمائیم نَعمآءِ تو نامُتِناهی اَست وَ شُکرانهٔ ما مَحدود چِگونِه مَحدود شُکرِ غیرِ مَحدود نَمایَد عاجزیم از شُکرِ الطافِ تو وَ بِه کَمالِ عجز تَوَجُّه بِه مَلَکوتِ تو می نَمائیم وَ طَلَبِ اِزدیادِ نِعمَت وَ عَطایِ تو می کُنیم توئی دَهَندِه وَ بَخشَندِه وَ تَوانا

Arabic
A'rabí

عَرَبى

O Lord! Thou art the Remover of every anguish and the Dispeller of every affliction. Thou art He Who banisheth every sorrow and setteth free every slave, the Redeemer of every soul. O Lord! Grant deliverance through Thy mercy, and reckon me among such servants of Thine as have gained salvation.

The Báb

اللّهُمَّ اِنَّكَ اَنْتَ مُفَرِّجٌ كُلُّ هَمٍّ وَ مُنْقِضٌ كُلُّ كَرْبٍ وَ مُذْهِبٌ كُلُّ غَمٍّ وَ مُخَلِّصٌ كُلُّ عَبْدٍ وَ مُنْقِذٌ كُلُّ نَفْسٍ خَلِّصْنِى اللّهُمَّ بِرَحْمَتِكَ وَ اَجْعَلْنِى مِنْ عِبَادِكَ المُنْقَذِينَ.

Is there any Remover of difficulties save God?
Say: Praised by God! He is God!
All are his servants and all abide by His bidding!

The Báb

هَلْ مِن مُفَرِّجٍ غَيرُاللّه قُلْ سُبْحَانَ اللّه
هُوَ اللّه
كُلٌّ عِبادٌ لَهُ وَ كُلٌّ بِأمرِهِ قائِمُون.

Pronunciation Guide

Farsi	Englisi	Pronunciation
اَ	a	**a**nt
آ	á	**a**rm
ب	b	**b**at
د	d	**d**og
ف	f	**f**ast
گ	g	**g**o
ه	h	**h**at
ح	ḣ	**h**at
اِ	i	b**e**st
ی	í	m**ee**t
ج	j	**j**et
ک	k	**k**ey
ل	l	**l**ove
م	m	**m**int
ن	n	**n**ap
پ	p	**p**at
ق	q*	me**r**ci
ر	r	**r**un
س	s	**s**and
ص	ṡ	**s**and
ث	s̤	**s**and

Farsi	Englisi	Pronunciation
ت	th	**t**ool
ط	t	**t**ool
اُ	u	sh**o**rt
و	ú	m**oo**n
و	v	**v**erb
ی	y	**y**es
ذ	dh	**z**ero
ض	d	**z**ero
ز	z	**z**ero
ظ	ż	**z**ero
چ	ch	**ch**air
غ	gh*	me**r**ci
خ	kh*	ba**ch**
ش	sh	**sh**are
ژ	zh	plea**s**ure
ع	'	uh-oh†

Vowels

Farsi	Englisi	Pronunciation
اَ	a	**a**nt
آ	á	**a**rm
اِ	i	b**e**st
ی	í	m**ee**t
اُ	u	sh**o**rt
و	ú	m**oo**n

* guttural sound from back of throat
† Glottal stop, breathing pause

-16-

The Persian Alphabet

We want to simplify your Persian learning journey as it is such a unique & enigmatic language. There are 32 official Persian letters. The letters change form depending on their position in a word or when they appear separate from other letters. For example, the letter ghayn غ has four ways of being written depending on where it appears in any given word:

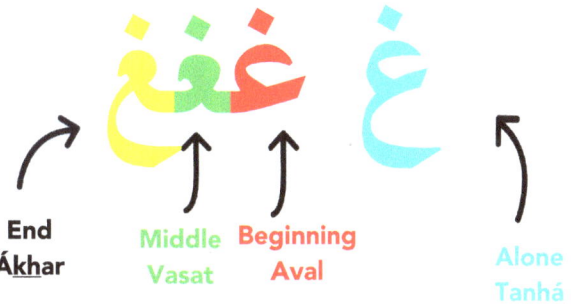

End — Ákhar
Middle — Vasat
Beginning — Aval
Alone — Tanhá

It is important to note that Persian books are read from right to left (←). There are 7 separate/stand-alone letters that do not connect in the same way to adjacent letters (these will be depicted in blue). They are:

Stand alone — Tanhá vámístan

The short vowels a, i & u are usually omitted in literature and are depicted by markings above & below letters (◌َ). They are not allocated a letter name, unlike their long vowel counterparts á: alef, í: ye & ú: váv (و ی آ).

Additional Letter & Symbol of note:

◌ّ = double letter   ◌ً = letter n   لا = l + á (lá)   اى = á   اِی = í
ىٰ = á   ـُو = ú   ◌ْ = '   ـِی = í   ـِ = í   ـَىْ = ay   ـَیْ = ay   ـَوْ = aw   ـُوْ = aw

Persian Alphabet Letter Guide

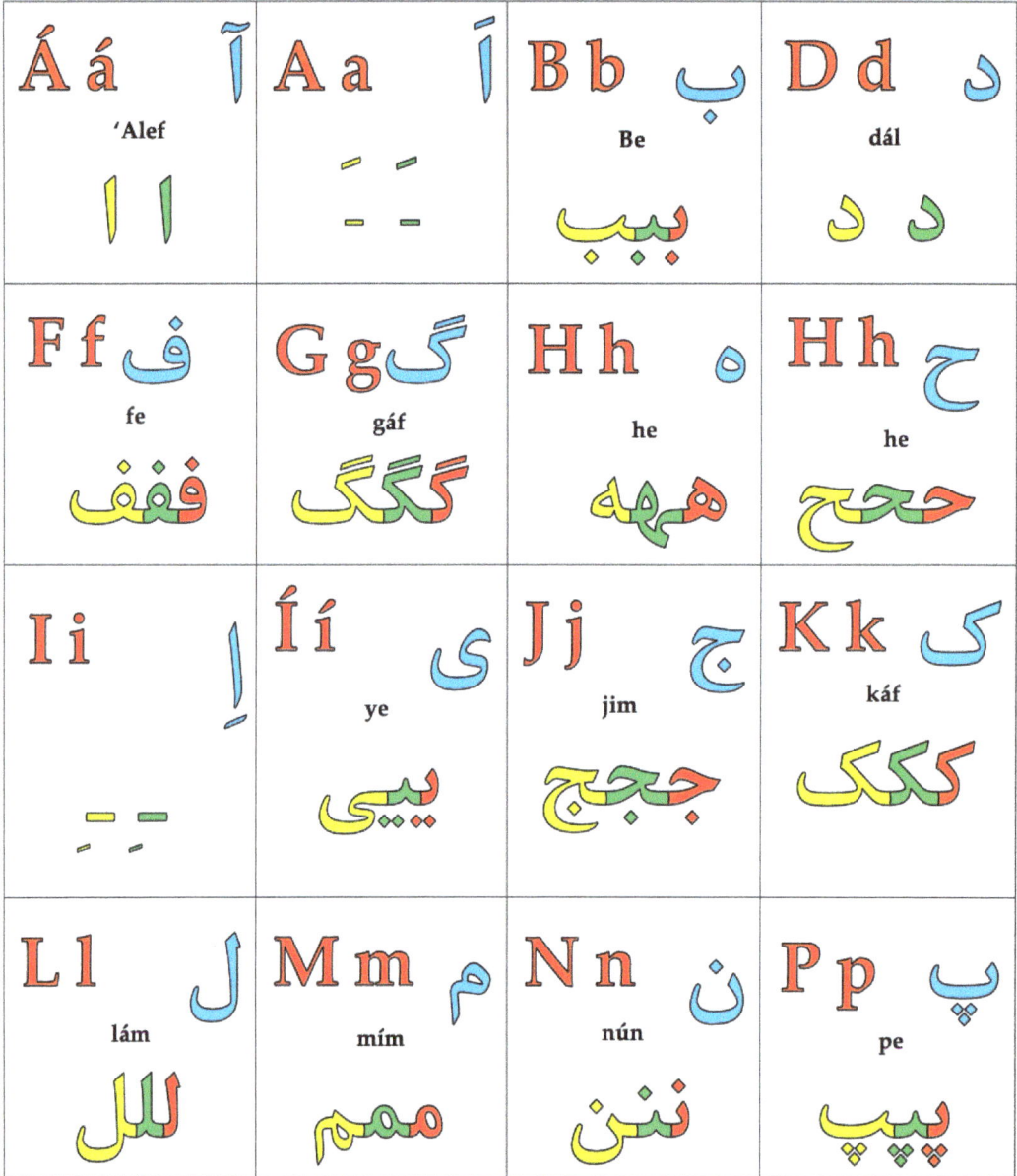

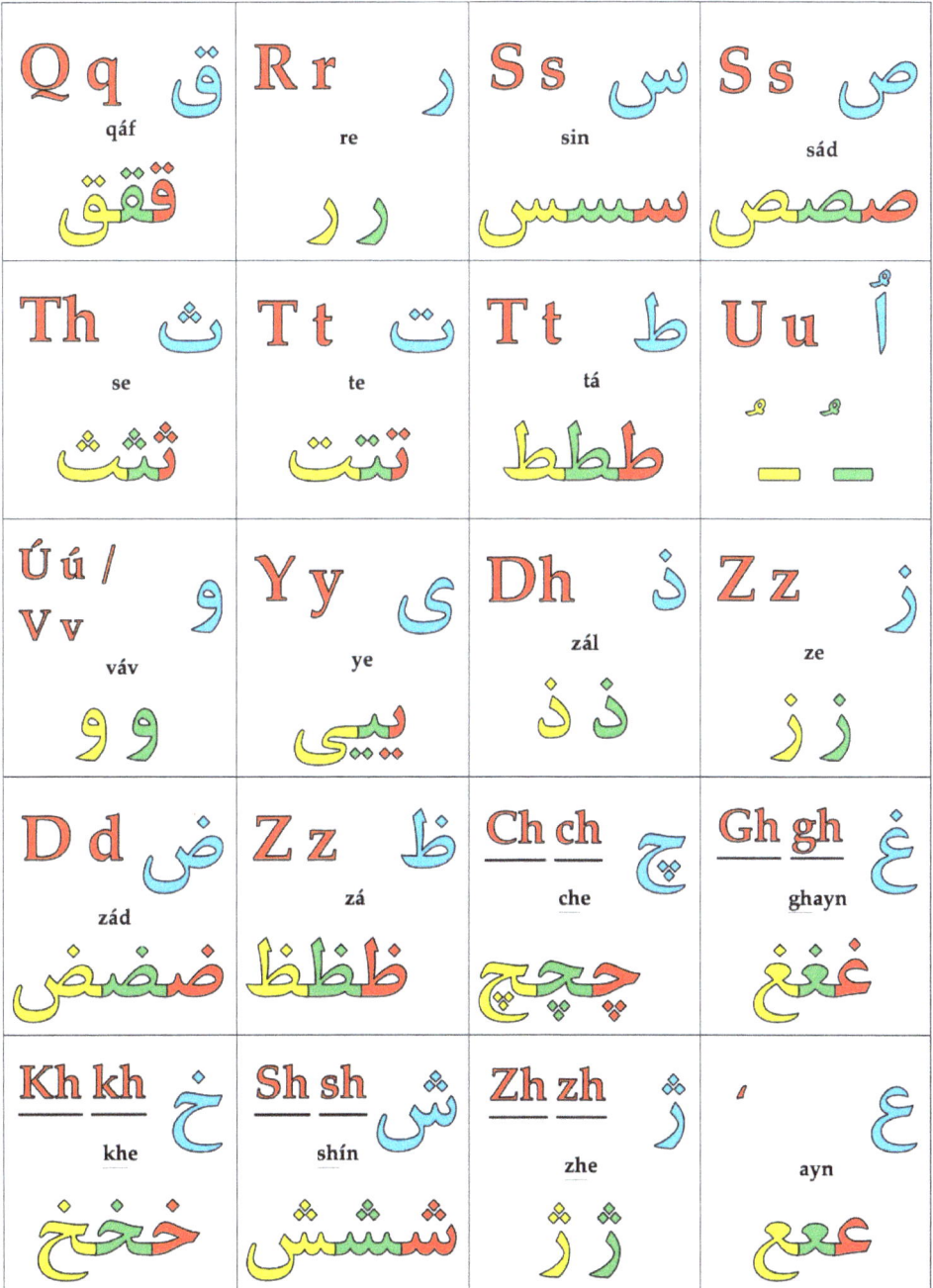

Need help reading or decoding the words?

**Make it easier, Download our Digital Poster Bahá'í Persian Alphabet guide printable:
Go to this link and use free code.**

CODE: BAHAIPRAYER